Being Successful In Today's Ever Changing Job Market

Today's Ever Changing Job Market

Companies everywhere are looking for a new type of employee. Companies want an employee who is agile, focused on reducing costs and adding value to the organization. Companies are no longer looking for the employee with ten to twenty years of experience only. With the market changing and with the requirements most organizations are looking for changing, we as job seekers must change as well. In this short book, I want to take the time to highlight what I have seen as a millennial in today's job market. I want to provide you with the tools necessary to be successful at a time where getting a job is similar to playing the lottery in a sense. I want you to be successful in your career and I hope this book helps.

Chapter 1 – Applying for Jobs in Today's Market

You are sitting at home and you power up your laptop and go straight to one of the top job sites on the internet. The list includes Indeed, Monster, and CareerBuilder to name a few. You went to college and have a Bachelor's degree in Business or Criminal Justice or Engineering. No matter what the degree field you went in, you are finally ready to begin your job search and here you are. Sitting at your computer ready to type in the key words that will assist you in finding your new job. Now how you search for a job initially is going to be variable to where you are in your career. For instance, maybe you are a Baby Boomer or a Generation X job seeker with a few years of experience under your belt and you know the sort of jobs that you are looking for. However, maybe you are a Millennial with limited experience and are only focused on getting paid a substantial salary to help pay off student loans and do the "Adult" things you have to do after you graduate. Either way now is the time to enter those words, "accounting", "criminal justice", "sales manager", "financial analyst", "systems consultant", whatever the words are that you would utilize to start your search, you ENTER them. To your surprise hundreds or thousands of job opportunities are finally before you. Now this is where your decisions will greatly affect your success. Remember earlier I said the job market has changed. You no longer have the capabilities to be as "selective" initially. Now there is one caveat to that statement, if you already have a job that you love and you are simply doing some casual strolling within the job market you can be selective. However, for those of you who are in desperate need of a job now is not the time to go through and read every single job description within the search results. So what do you do? YOU APPLY FOR AS MANY AS YOU CAN. That is correct, you apply for as many of the jobs that are on the search engine as you can. Why would you do such a thing? Well in today's job market, I am a firm believer that selectively applying for jobs will not work. The market has changed. Organizations receive thousands of applications for roles and trust me you are just a number in the many. Now, I plan on changing that for you later on in this book. However, as of right now, you are just a number. During this application frenzy you should also take the time do determine if there are specific organizations that would be a great place for you to work. For instance, some finance majors may have 2 banks that they would DIE to work for. If immediately you have a couple of organizations that come to mind, go directly to their website and sign up to apply for jobs on their sites directly. Now keep in mind the application frenzy will CONTINUE. That is correct. Yes, you read my last statement correctly ladies and gentlemen. The application frenzy occurs on those organizations sites as well. That means FINANCE majors, IT gurus, and account managers, you have to apply for a lot of jobs that may not be your IDEAL job. My guess is if an organization is on your top 2 list, that it is on the list of many others as well. So, take the time to apply for jobs that may be somewhat outside of your scope. Apply for literally as many jobs as you can on their website. The great news about applying for a ton of jobs during this initial job search is that organizations know what they are looking for in a candidate. Let them determine who is a great fit for a role. Your job is to put your application in. I recommend to everyone I talk to, around 10-100 applications a day is ideal. There are sites where you can apply directly from their site to the job posting (CareerBuilder and Indeed) are great examples and this allows for mass applications. I remember when I was fresh out of college and I was job hunting, I went on CareerBuilder and uploaded my resume and did mass applications to multiple jobs all at once. I also spent some time applying for jobs on Indeed and other job search sites. I probably applied for 100+ jobs and was able to land 5 interviews in one day. Needless to say, I was able to secure a job during that one day of mass interviews. If you are only willing to apply for 1 job per day, I would expect that the number of interviews or call backs will be limited for you. Again, you are not the only one applying for these jobs (unless the job was recommended to you by the hiring manager directly).

Chapter 2 – How quickly are the denials coming through?

Now here comes the true test. You have been applying daily for jobs. Over the course of a couple of weeks you are sure you have applied for at least 50-100 jobs. The test isn't always that you have gotten call backs from the organizations human resources department. Now don't get me wrong, that test is a valid one and if you are getting those call backs then consider yourself on track to a successfully ending storyline. However, another test is if you are getting those pesky DENIAL emails within a few hours of submitting your job application. If that is the case there are a few things that you have to defiantly work on. Now my statements after this point are assuming that the jobs you are applying for are within your reach. For instance, if you are fresh out of college applying for a Financial Management job or a Director level role, you may want to be more realistic and focus your search criteria to entry level roles. If for any reason you have being applying for jobs that are far outside your reach then can you please rewind NOW. Start over from the very beginning of this book and start applying for jobs that are realistic depending on your level of expertise in the industry or area you are focused on. Ok, now we can get back to focusing on the individuals who have been applying for jobs that closely aligns to their experience and skill sets, but have still been getting those dreadful DENIAL emails. The first thing I will suggest is confirming the font that you are utilizing within your resume. Large companies now are utilizing filtering tools and mechanisms to eliminate a large portion of applications before they even reach human resources and one of the criteria could be FONT. Now instead of boring you with a lot on this subject let me keep this extremely simple. Consider using Garamond, Arial, or Calibri. There are tons of google discussions around this very topic so if you google "the best fonts to use on a resume" you will get a wide selection. However, one font that SHOULD NOT be on the list of considerations is TIMES NEW ROMAN. Yes you heard me correctly, DO NOT USE TIMES NEW

ROMAN on your job application. If you see any search that you do on the "best fonts to use" saying to use TIMES NEW ROMAN leave that site immediately and block it from every popping up in another one of your search options going forward. The last thing you want to do is have your application skipped over because of a font issue. This one is too easy to NOT FIX. Next on the list of possibilities will be one that you have probably heard a billion times and unfortunately I am going to say it again. Use key words and phrases in your resume. Now, every job is looking for a group of different skill sets; however, there are some key words that will make every application successful. I will spare you the time of going through a billion of these key words and phrases in this book; however, I will give you a few examples.

These include:

EXCELLENT COMMUNICATION SKILLS, GREAT LISTENING SKILLS, SUCCESSFULLY LEAD IMPLEMENTATIONS OR PROCESS IMPROVEMENT INITIATIVES, COLLABORATION, TIME MANAGEMENT,

CUSTOMER SERVICE FOCUSED, ABLE TO BUILD LASTING RELATIONSHIPS, SUCCESSFULLY MANAGED A TEAM OF 10, ABLE TO MASTER TECHNOLOGY QUICKLY, GREAT PROBLEM SOLVING ABILITY.

Ok, great. By now you should have the idea. These key words and phrases can go in the beginning of your resume prior to getting to your education and experience. Keep in mind as you are applying for jobs, there will be those positions that sound so enticing to you that you would do anything to get hired, for those jobs you should read through the job description and tie your experience back to the job description as much as possible. This leads me to my next topic of discussion.

I just gave you some of the simple things you should modify on your resume if you are getting lots of denials on job applications almost immediately after you apply (I consider that, denials within the first 24 hours of applying). However, there are a few other things that I want all of you to consider including in your resume and your application. A LinkedIn page or a page similar to

LinkedIn. If you have the time and are creative enough, creating your own webpage that highlights some of your experience, interests and information your family will be a great addition to your resume. Now for those who do not want to go this far, adding a link to your LinkedIn page will suffice. However, trust me if a potential employer can go to a webpage that you created that tells them a little bit about you on both a professional and personal level you are really making yourself stand out greatly from the crowd. The great news with this is that once its complete you really don't have to make many changes to it going forward. This was something that I did early on in my career and I was able to get a lot of positive feedback along the way. I put information about my favorite basketball team and my favorite player (the Chicago Bulls when my favorite player Michael Jordan played for them). I added highlight videos from his career. I added pictures from my college graduation and some other key events in my life. It didn't go into providing a family lineage but it provided the potential employer with information about me on both a professional and personal level. Of course, on this webpage was also a page that had my resume and the details of my experience as well. Again, the job market is not the same as it was many years ago and the only way to put a face with a name in today's job market is a website of some sort.

The next thing to discuss with you is providing a cover letter and some other supporting documents that could be extremely useful during an application process. Please keep in mind that some of these are customizable and some can be fairly generic to all applications. Depending on your level of interest, this will determine the level of effort you place on each application submittal. The first thing is the cover letter. MAKE YOUR COVER LETTER STAND OUT. Make the name of the cover letter John Smith, YOUR ONLY CHOICE or John Smith, COMPANY NAME. These are things you hear all the time so make sure you do them in the cover letter if you provide one. Now for the details inside the cover letter. I recommend you have one generic cover letter that you can add to any application as you are applying for jobs. This cover letter should be simple. I have provided an example of a generic cover letter at the end of this book for your reference. These are the types of cover letters that you can add to all applications and highlight some of your key skills. Keep in mind that if you are applying for a job that you are highly interested in I would change the generic cover letter to something more specific to the role at hand.

Fourth (after you discuss font, key phrases and words, and cover letter), providing a document shows the audience why you are the candidate they should chose. This document will highlight how your experience aligns with the requirements of the role as well as what some of your key strengths are. Now this document is fairly simple and I have provided a great example at the end of this book for your reference. Now for the strengths that you want to highlight, this information can be obtained by using Google and searching for "Strength Finder Tests". I have a book titled Strength Finder by Tom Rath that provides an assessment at the end. However, there are free tools available online as well. Either should suffice. The key here is to gather those key strengths you have and then highlighting those items on a separate document. I know this may seem like an awful lot but rest assured this information is going to make you stand out from the crowd. Maybe these ideas have sparked some ideas that are even better; however, the objective is the same. You want to stand out from the CROWD of individuals seeking the SAME job you are.

Chapter 3 – Human Resources preliminary interview

In this final chapter we will discuss how to get past the initial human resources interview. You have worked hard applying for hundreds of job applications and you have followed all the steps that I have outlined in this book so far. You are finally receiving emails from human resources to discuss the opportunity that you applied for in more detail. This is the time for you to begin your STUDYING of the role and the organization. The great thing about the preliminary interview with human resources is that it is

OVER THE PHONE. First do some research on the organization that you have applied for. If there is one thing I am almost positive will occur, especially for your larger organizations, is that human resources will ask you what you know about the organization. Now, each individual will have their preference for what they discuss during this 1 to 2 minute discussion. I focus on the number of employees that work at the organization, the services provided to the customers of this organization, and the revenue and growth of the company to date. Why do I chose these items? Mostly because they are important to me. If you are looking at an organization and you notice steady decline in revenue and growth or stead layoffs in the industry it is a little concerning and is something you will need to consider during these discussions with the company. For instance, if the organization laid off 10% of its workforce last year you may want to know if there is the potential for more layoffs based on the current performance of the company. If you are in desperate need of a job and it concerns you but you want to leave it as an optional opportunity then you should factor that in to your salary negotiations and what you are willing to make now and be ok getting laid off in a year. Jot down the information that you want to discuss with human resources about the organization and rehearse (YES REHEARSE) how you will present it on the call. Another topic that gets discussed on this call is salary. I will say this now and move on, DO NOT PROVIDE YOUR CURRENT OR MOST RECENT SALARY information to HR. That information is your confidential information and you are not obligated to disclose it. Some human resources representatives may not like this and press you for your current salary information. You will need to judge how important a job is to you and how risky you are willing to be with the opportunity on the table. If the human resources representative is not willing to accept your response (which I will get into momentarily), then you may have to provide the information. However, I recommend you say the following, "I have been told by my accountant to not provide the details of my salary; however, I am currently looking for a range of around $85,000 depending on the total package the company is providing". This keeps it fairly simple and lets the human resources representative know the most important information and that is what dollar amount are you willing to leave your current organization for.

The final piece of information that the human resources representative will want to know more about is your previous experience and your most current experience. The best way to discuss your experience as a whole is to start with your previous experience, then discuss your current role, and finally tie all that up with the role you are currently applying for. Prior to the phone interview, when the human resources representative first contacts you, be sure to provide them with the document that highlights your strengths and highlights how your experience mirrors the role that you have applied for (again, there is an example at the end of the book for you to preview). For instance, if the job is extremely customer centric and wants someone who can provide exceptional customer service, then you want to highlight how you have provided that in your current and previous roles. You could say:

> In my previous role I focused on providing exceptional customer service to our business operations team by ensuring they had a seamless system experience, in my current role I was able to really hone in on that customer service focus by providing great customer service to the executives that utilize our current SharePoint system. That is why I applied for this Customer Service Management position, I feel that my experience working with customers at all levels within an organization successfully has prepared me to lead a team and ensure they are providing an exceptional level of customer service as well.

I know it may sound simple but it is something that will allow you to stand out from some in the preliminary stage of the interview. Please keep in mind that during this time you may be ask more technical related questions or additional general questions. The key in all of these questions is to understand the organization and the role and always tie your answers back to some key components discussed in the job description. The human resources preliminary interview is extremely important because they hold the key to the hiring manager. You have to impress this individual and if you can even capture a few of the recommendations that I have provided in your preliminary interview you should be able to get a second interview with the hiring manager.

More To Come

I know that I have poured a lot out at once to you guys. I hope that you can begin to implement some of these recommendations into your day to day job search. I know I have said it a lot, but the job market has truly changed and it is extremely important to ensure that you are standing out along the way. Companies are looking for individuals who are agile and willing to do whatever it takes to get a job done. That doesn't always mean you have to work 60 or more hours a week, but it does mean that you have to do things differently than would have been expected in the past. This methodology even stands true in how you apply for jobs in today's market. These simple modifications during a job search could be all it takes to get you in the door. I hope this short book was impactful and helpful to you. I plan on continuing these short books and my next one will be on how to wow them during an interview. If you are able to get through all the preliminary activities and you have an interview setup with the hiring manager, this is the time to SEAL THE DEAL. I will provide you with some of the things I would recommend you do during that interview that will have you standing out from the crowd. Thanks again, for allowing me to provide you with some valuable information and I hope you return for the next book to come.

Appendix

Generic Simple Cover Letter Example

Human Resources

To whom it may concern:

Are you looking for an individual with:

- A Bachelor's Degree in Accounting and a Master's in Business Administration?
- Thorough problem solving and analytical skills?
- Excellent written and oral communication skills, which focus on thorough listening skills?
- Prior experience with ecommerce implementations, vendor portal implementations, UAT, test script creation?
- Great problems solving abilities?
- Experience implementing new systems and implementing system enhancements.
- Exceptional ability to work with a wide array of individuals?
- Successfully implemented many process improvements and efficiencies?
- Great at multi-tasking?
- Thorough experience data mining, running queries, and creating reports?
- A passion to learn and increase the skills I have?
- A self-starter who is willing to do whatever it takes to get the job done right?

If so, then you need look no further. You will see from my enclosed resume that I meet all of these qualifications and more.

I would very much like to discuss my opportunities with **your company.** To schedule an interview, please call me at 000-000-000. You can give me a call at any time during the day, if you do not get me immediately leave a message and I will call you back

Thank you for taking the time to review my resume. I look forward to hearing from you.

Sincerely,

Your Name

Example of how to show you are the candidate to choose for the job

Your Name, MBA
Your Address
000-000-0000

WHY I AM THE CANDIDATE OF CHOICE

YOUR REQUIREMENTS	MY EXPERIENCE
Advanced degree, such as an MBA or Masters in Information Security	Bachelor's Degree in Accounting – **** **College** Masters of Business Administration (MBA) – **** **University**
Demonstrated ability to develop and maintain good working relationships with internal and external customers	On a daily basis in my current role I successfully work effectively with a wide array of individuals within the workplace. Those individuals have included vice presidents, directors, managers, and coworkers. – ****companies you did these items at******
Demonstrated functional audit knowledge and ability to apply auditing protocols	Thorough understanding of audit procedures and a keen ability to determine potential areas of risk involved with a particular process or control. Also, able to make independent decisions based on audit findings without being persuaded by key stakeholders involved in a specific process. ****companies you did these items at******
Demonstrated ability to reason logically, analyze data presented, evaluate the impact of information collected, and draw appropriate conclusions	Consistently working on projects that require thorough analysis and exceptional problem solving skills. For instance, currently in my role I am required to analyze data on a continual basis and assist end users in resolving their issues within our Supply Chain systems ****companies you did these items at******
Demonstrated ability to communicate clearly, concisely, and accurately using oral and written communications with various levels of management	Excellent written communication skills which stem from my minor in English ****companies you did these items at****** Excellent oral communication skills that stems from my focus on listening to the issue or situation at hand. Great listening skills allow me to have great oral communication skills.

MY TOP FIVE STRENGTHS (provided by assessment within *Strength Finder 2.0* by Tom Rath)

COLLABORATION	Strong team player – always willing to help others in need and interacting with all levels of the organization. We all have one thing in common; to provide quality customer service to our internal customers as well as our external customers.
ACCOUNTABILITY	Takes responsibility and ownership for my work and anything I commit to whether large or small. Commit to stable values such as honesty and loyalty. Have a good follow through to completion.
ARRANGER	Great organizer; when faced with complex situations involving many factors, I enjoy managing all of the variables, aligning and realigning them until I am sure I have arranged them in the most productive way possible.
ANALYTICAL	Have strong "Prove It" skills. Always support my decision based on the facts. I am very detail oriented and have the ability to think about all the factors that might affect a situation.
ACHIEVER	Have a great deal of stamina and work hard. I take great satisfaction from being busy and productive. Love new challenges.

The End (until next time)

www.ingramcontent.com/pod-product-compliance
Lightning Source LLC
Chambersburg PA
CBHW050433180526
45159CB00006B/2525